# Poetry

AF373553

# *Poetry*

## Fun with Pencils!

## K.A. Smith

KeVision Books

# *Poetry: Fun with Pencils!*

This is a work of fiction. Names, characters, places, and
incidents are products of the authors' imag-
ination or are
used fictitiously. Any resemblance to actual
persons, living or
dead, or to events or locales, is entirely coinci-
dental.
Poetry: Fun with Pencils!
Copyright © 2024 by Kevin A. Smith and
KeVision Books
No part of this publication may be reproduced,
stored in a
retrieval system, or transmitted in any form or
by any means-
electronic, mechanical, digital, photocopy,
recording, or any
other-except for brief quotations in printed
reviews, without
the prior permission of the publisher.

# Contents

# Poetry: Fun with Pencils!

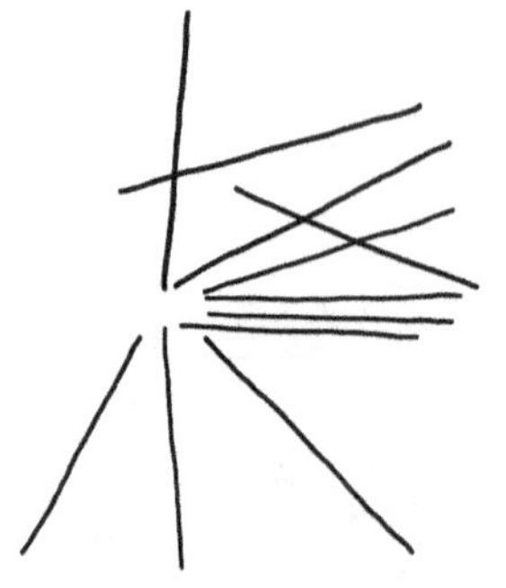

# Sunset or Sunrise

Sunset or sunrise
Is beautiful in either eye?
"...Half full or half empty," someone said.
Maybe they are in the same lie.

I would contest it then
To see which one wins.
I found myself refereeing,
In the middle.
I'm in.

# Grass Along the Road

Grass along the road
Looks as they drive,
Giving company like fellows
On a long ride.

The grass waves with attention
In the corner of eyes.
It's like a parade sometimes,
A unique guide.

# A Breakthrough

A breakthrough sort of looks like this
In the mind, once a person finds.
With a release of air and sharp intelligences,
It tingles and begins.
The feeling of celebration is kin.

The hill seats beneath finally!
First thoughts wander
To someone special in the family.
Should you know the trust?
Invisible, it hides above.
When unnoticed, it could cut.

# The "Putting" Flag

The "putting" flag wags happily
As the wind blows with excitement!
In the distance, a loud wack sounds before
A golfer yells, alerting those waiting
For what's instored.

On the final hole,
The "putting" flag stays in the plays.
The wind continues.
It's an obstacle for the one holding...
At this special venue.

# In the Stands

In the stands,
Memories.
Games fitted for romance and...
A lonely mind.
A person creates company.
A fun neighbor pushes kind.
Out of the eye,
Someone lovely
Says hi.

# It's Camping Outdoors

It's camping outdoors,
Expressed in the shadows.
Tinting with fun.
Shadows and the light
Are as one.

Where is the other camp?
A shadow
Coming from the lamp.
It reaches from afar,
Having fun.
Are we as they are?

# Ew!

Ew! It looks away,
Afraid of something
That smells!
Like covered in gel,
It irks uncomfortably,
The mail!

# Here's a Gift

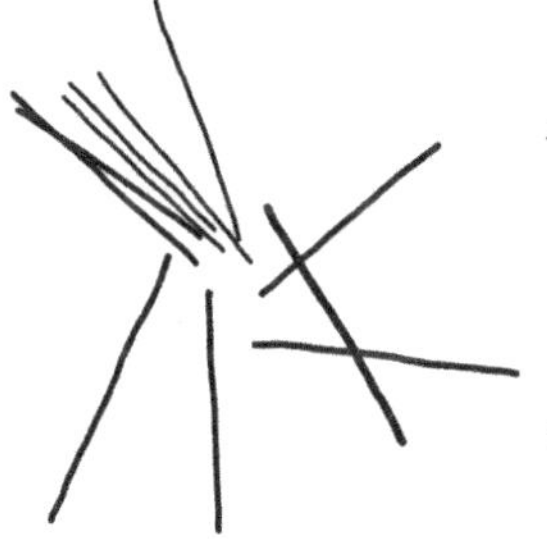

Here's a gift.
A symbol of my gratitude.
A strand for now.
My hair is in good care.
Today, I can take a bow.

A special gift it is.
Whoever handles will live.
Be thoughtful of pows.
If cut to pieces,
It's out.

# Fishy Don't Tell

What a big mouth it has.
That fish will be the last
I tell a secret
That is sad.

What big eyes it has,
Like looking through glass,
It shows and...
Reflects a boat in Trinidad.

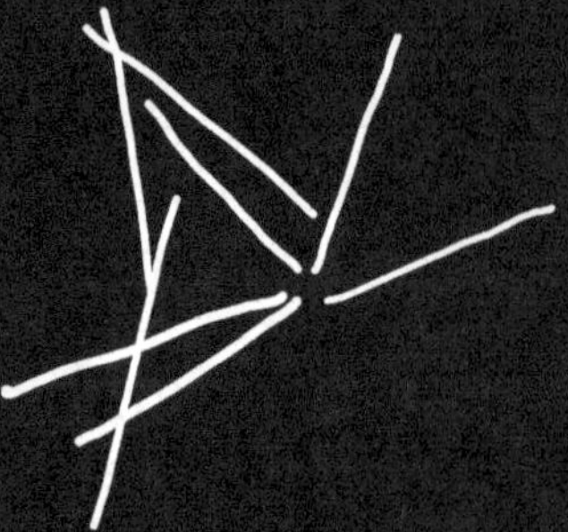

# The Hand

Away you!
Get the clue.
Don't stay!
Do what the hand say.

The fingers are like bars.
It senses if approached.
They'll grow tall like a wall,
Averting the person's fall.

# Whiskers on a Flower

Whiskers on a flower
Would be sensible.
Bouquets are norm.
Like a cat, they could react.
They could inform.

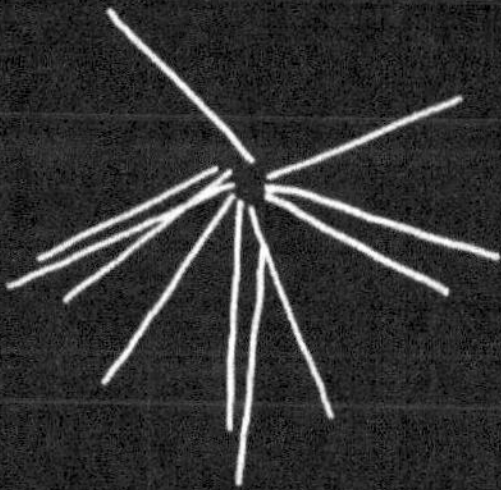

# Grand Jeté

Grand Jeté!
A ballerina jumps out of the way
Just in time.
With grace and harmony,
The ballerina dodges the crime.
Give her a standing... olay!

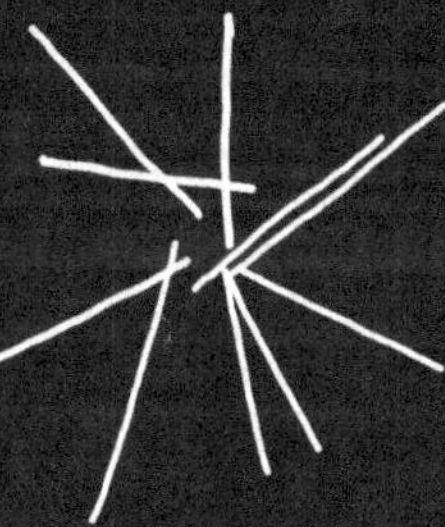

# Something is Laughing

This something is laughing
At my words.
I won't get discouraged
Being picked
By a funny looking bird.

# Five Track Runners

Five track runners
Running at the speed of light,
Makes a sharp turn.
I fear for their life.

A turn of momentum,
Two posts in...
Goals need to be accomplished.
Who will win?

# Sun on a Glass Cup

Sun on a glass cup,
A beautiful collection.
A vision of ice cubes
Would be cool.
A nice reflection.

Remaining by the window,
Frosted as the bubbles climb.
"Waiter, I would like a lime."
Late in time, heat gains
And coldness becomes the blame.

# Wearing a Glove

Wearing a glove,
For a reach that is steep.
I don't know what lies
Beneath.

Something touched the surface
Of my thoughts at an angle.
I defy,
I wrangle.

# Night Lights

The night light is on
Whoever's behind the sun is having fun.
It's a mystic scene
Like stage lights, he brings
Excitement and contentment.
The night light yields
As a player displays
Self-determined on the field.
Everyone has chills.

# By the Pond

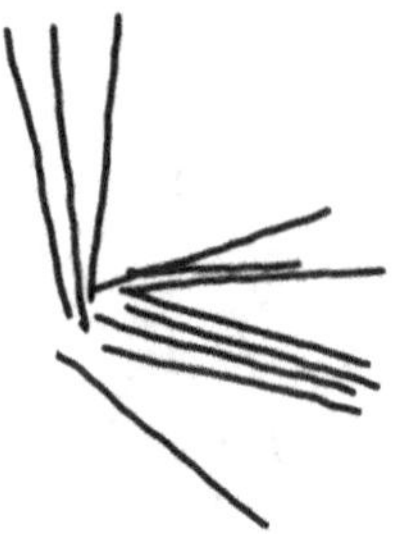

By the pond, ducks appear.
I'm fond of the tall stems
Sitting near, so relaxing.
In the company of nature,
I'm basking.

# A Volcano

A volcano erupts...
And sends smoke very much.
In the distance, I will stay.
Out of harm's way is a brighter day.
A tour like this is not a common wish,
But its memory will be on my list.

# The Windup

The windup is here.
It whistles with gust.
A rope goes around and around.
With a hook, it's throwed near.
At the end was a rescue
A proud moment of kindness
A person was gifted something.
The finest.

# In Disbelief

Slouched with its jaw dropped
In disbelief...
A surprise was sure it would be.
Mouth wide open like a cup,
It didn't notice something flying in.
It's bad luck.

# A Boatride on a River

A boatride on a river heads for an adventure.
Between water waves and mountains,
The boat rocks while the paddlers enjoy a fountain.
The rest is over in "secs."
It's time for the next obstacle.
A big crest.

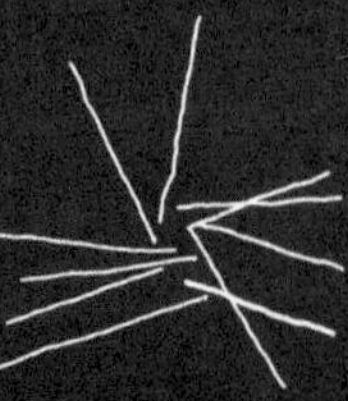

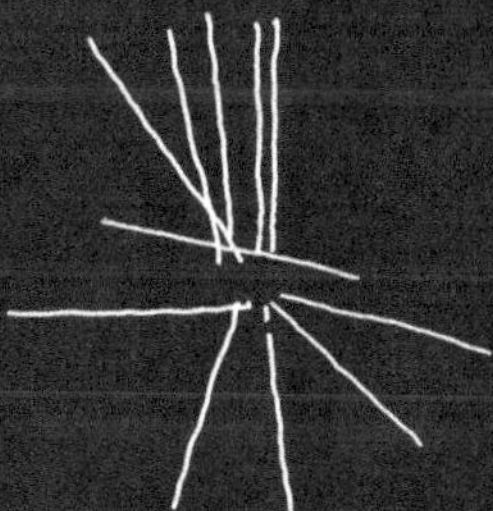

# A Man in a Top Hat

A man in a top hat points the way
In the direction someone needs
To go and stay.
The hat is complimented,
For its stripes felt secure.
A person with a hat like this is...
Always sure?

# The Life of a Bug

The life of a bug is loved.
Going from limb to limb,
It crawls, flies, and hugs.
It's a tiny note that sits on leaves.
Where would we be without the anecdote,
"Bee at ease."

# The Mighty One

The mighty one is poised.
It sits as though
Knowledge is the flow...
I keep my distance from the annoy.
I'm coy.

# The Stars and the Mountains

The stars and the mountains.
What a wonderful scene.
A backdrop of light and tails
Streaks across the top of a mighty rock.
Very well.

My lens loves the relection
And the glare.
If I had to pick, it would be a shop.
The stars or the mountains?
The mood is a groove.
Don't choose.

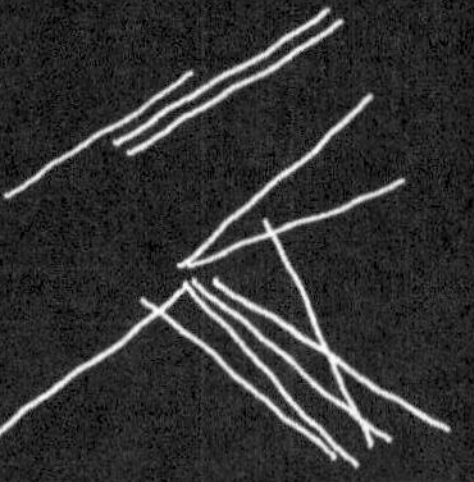

# The Backsack

Loads on the back
Will crack.
It would be wise to...
Lightly pack the sack.

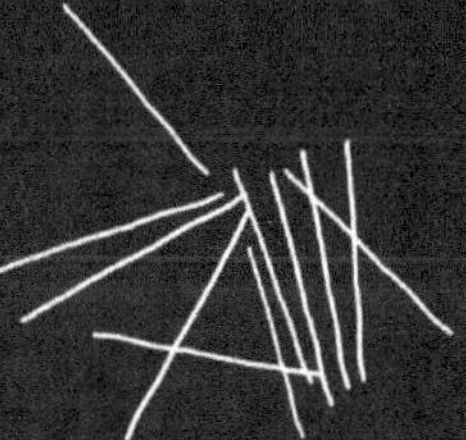

# Superhero

It's a superhero.
What will it do?
When the dream is attached,
A cape appears on the back.

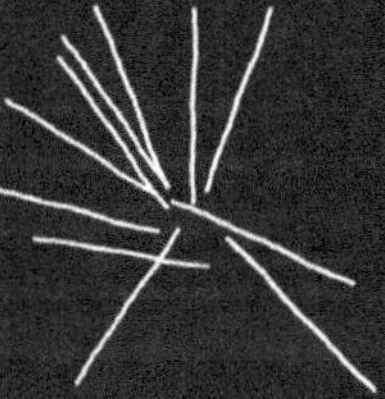

# Placing a Cone

Placing a cone in front is blunt.
The obstacle is fun, but not free.
The hand as a tool, the cone, is placed.
And the...
A world becomes noticeable.
A fool of me.

# A Unique Pose

A unique pose it is.
The person leans on a support
That feels like a fork!
The arms stretched wide
With it under, the photographer
Makes a mistake.
What a blunder.

# I'm Thirsty

It's thirsty!
A long tongue sticks out.
From the beak, it takes a lick
of freshness for the weak.

The hair stands when complete.
It's time for another adventure,
But first...
Wait with the fleet.
Thirst.

# "X" Marks the Spot

"X" marks the spot,
The weather is hot.
No one stands except me.
Alone, I'll go home
Without praise in the vicinity.
Only the money.

# On One Leg

On one leg,
An artwork is balanced.
Sold in a gallery,
"I like this one."
"How much?"
"It fits me."
The puzzle has no feet.

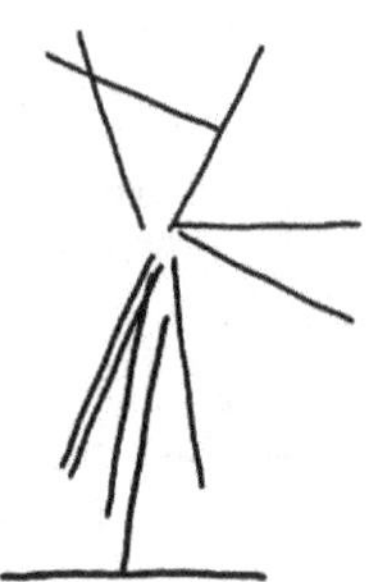

# The Tent

The tent of a festival is held
By the performances it sells.
Go everywhere.
There're elephants, lions, and tigers.
Monkey around and jump through hoops.
Did you see the flyer?

# Hairless Brush

A brush's hair needs care.
It's losing. Quickly!
Go find replacements
At a store over there!

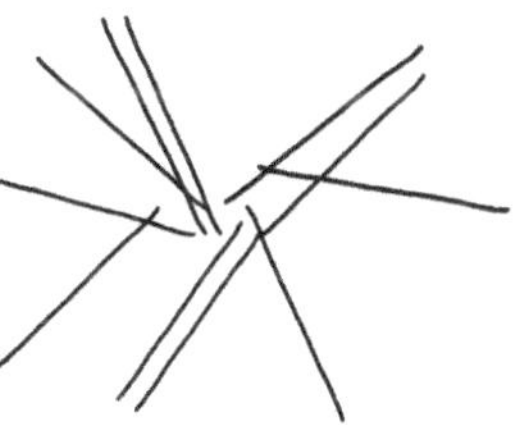

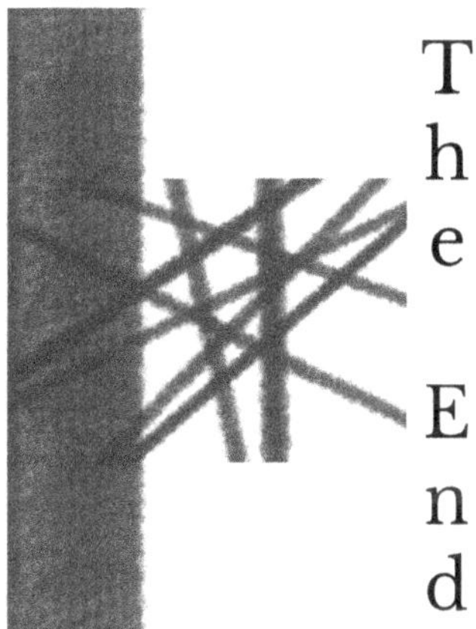

# Dedication

To all the loved ones.

www.ingramcontent.com/pod-product-compliance
Lightning Source LLC
Chambersburg PA
CBHW061329140726
47998CB00007B/2622